Corporate Tax Shelters in a Global Economy

AEI STUDIES ON TAX REFORM
Kevin A. Hassett
Series Editor

Corporate Tax Shelters in a Global Economy

Why They Are a Problem and What We Can Do about It

Daniel N. Shaviro

The AEI Press

Publisher for the American Enterprise Institute

WASHINGTON, D.C.

Available in the United States from the AEI Press, c/o Client Distribution Services, 193 Edwards Drive, Jackson, TN 38301. To order, call toll free: 1-800-343-4499. Distributed outside the United States by arrangement with Eurospan, 3 Henrietta Street, London WC2E 8LU, England.

Library of Congress Cataloging-in-Publication Data

Shaviro, Daniel N.
    Corporate tax shelters in a global economy : why they are a problem and what we can do about it/
        Daniel N. Shaviro.
        p. cm.
    Includes bibliographical references.
    ISBN 0-8447-7182-1 (pbk. : alk. paper)
1. Corporations—Taxation. 2. Tax shelters. I. Title.

    HD2753.A3S35 2004
    336.24'316'0973—dc22

                                                    2004021829

10 09 08 07 06 05 04   1 2 3 4 5 6 7

Printed in the United States of America

Contents

Foreword

Economists have reached a broad consensus concerning the appearance of an optimal tax system. Such a system would have a very broad base—perhaps limited to consumption—and marginal tax rates as low as revenue demands will allow. While there is general agreement concerning those basic features of an optimal tax system, significant disagreement remains concerning the size of the benefits to be gained from a fundamental reform that would replace the current system of high marginal tax rates with one that conformed closely to the prescriptions of theory. Disagreement also abounds concerning the distributional impact of fundamental tax reforms. The lack of professional consensus undoubtedly discourages would-be reformers, who for more than a decade have shied away from fundamental fixes and instead tinkered endlessly with a system that has increased steadily in complexity.

With this state of affairs in mind, we at AEI have organized a tax reform seminar series since January 1996. At each seminar, an economist presents original research designed to bring consensus concerning the costs and benefits of fundamental tax reform one step closer. Recent topics include transition problems in moving to a consumption tax, the effects of consumption taxation on housing and the stock market, the distributional impact of tax reforms, the effect of privatizing Social Security on the long-term budget outlook, and the international tax implications of fundamental reform.

The goal of this pamphlet series is to distribute the best research on economic issues in tax reform to as broad an audience as possible. Each publication reflects not only the insights of the authors, but also the helpful comments and criticisms of seminar participants—economists, attorneys, accountants, and journalists in the tax policy community.

Tax reform proposals often include alterations to the corporate tax code. There are two main motivations for this. First, taxes that treat consumption as the base require extensive revisions to existing law. Depreciation rules, for example, are often replaced with expensing provisions. Second, it is widely acknowledged that the complexity of our existing tax code encourages aggressive tax management or "evasion" activities. Reform proposals often seek to make the code simpler and more transparent.

Tax reform proposals generated by economists often assume that the legal aspects will miraculously work themselves out—that the reform, if enacted, will work exactly as planned. But can any tax system eliminate costly evasion activity? In this volume, AEI visiting scholar Daniel N. Shaviro explores the causes and costs of tax avoidance and provides a useful guide to the key conceptual issues that must be addressed in order to design a truly effective tax reform.

In the first chapter, Shaviro attempts to identify the specific aspects of U.S. tax law that lead to extensive "paper pushing" in the interest of tax minimization, as well as a metric by which a tax authority can establish whether a particular tax planning action should be considered abusive or wasteful. In the second chapter, Shaviro explores tax arbitrages that are common among U.S. multinationals and discusses their economic consequences. Throughout, the author discusses policies that can soften the economic blow from avoidance activities.

Any fundamental tax reform will require rules to ensure that taxpayers face the incentives that are intended by reformers. This volume is a valuable guide for those who must establish these rules.

KEVIN A. HASSETT
American Enterprise Institute

1

Are Corporate Tax Shelters an "Abuse" That Should Be Stopped?

Corporate tax sheltering is all over the news. CBS's *60 Minutes* had a story on it recently, as did PBS's *Crossfire*. Pulitzer Prize–winning *New York Times* reporter David Cay Johnston drew attention to the phenomenon, both in front-page articles in the *Times* and in his best-selling book, *Perfectly Legal*.

When the esoteric details of companies' financial transactions start attracting so much attention, it is natural to ask why. In this case, the main reasons are twofold. First, a lot of money is involved. Five years ago, Stanford law professor Joseph Bankman estimated the annual revenue cost to the U.S. Treasury of corporate tax shelters at $10 billion,[1] and there is reason to suspect that the current annual cost is even higher. Second, the corporate tax shelter issue has struck a public chord through its association with Enron-style financial accounting abuse.

Accusations of tax-planning "abuse" have naturally generated a backlash from the companies' (or their tax planners') defenders, who claim that they are merely engaged in legitimate tax planning, and cite the famous statement by Judge Learned Hand that "[a]nyone may arrange his affairs so that his taxes shall be as low as possible. . . . There is not even a patriotic duty to increase one's taxes."[2] Defenders of the transactions note as well that the corporate income tax is a highly flawed instrument, suggesting that perhaps we should not overly bemoan companies' success in avoiding it. In addition, the defenders emphasize the ambiguous character of the legal issues raised by borderline transactions. The typical corporate tax shelter transaction involves a lot of energetic paper shuffling to little or no economic effect, creating a favorable tax result if the rules are read literally but running afoul of general legal standards that require tax-effective transactions to meet minimum thresholds of a nontax business purpose and economic substance. Sometimes, there is reasonable disagreement about whether a given transaction actually does fail to meet these standards under existing law—although, as Professor Bankman notes, there often is little dispute that a given transaction, even if tax effective when done, permits a nonsensical result and therefore ought to be barred prospectively.[3] But, where a given transaction might work under present law, defenders argue, how can engaging in it be abusive?

This paper aims to provide a calmer, more rational assessment of the issues posed by corporate tax shelters than one can get by debating whether they involve "abuse." I argue that framing the debate in terms of "abusive" tax shelters versus "legitimate" tax planning is simply not coherent or useful. Energetic paper shuffling, while it can lead to a lot of waste, is not evil in and of itself, in the manner of violence or fraud, unless it involves a deliberate failure to heed existing law. Yet, even if corporate tax shelter transactions are not unmistakably "abusive" in the absence of a rule banning them—and whether there is or should be such a rule is precisely the thing being debated—I argue in this paper that they actually pose serious problems for the tax system and call for a substantial government response. Corporate tax shelters waste resources both directly, through the planning and transaction costs they entail, and indirectly, by making the tax system, flawed though it is, even less neutral economically than it would otherwise be. Therefore, paradoxically, an economic substance approach that impedes the shelters by making them costlier (and thus socially more wasteful) to engage in can actually reduce total waste by reducing their frequency.

So the underlying issue is more mundane—and complex—than sniffing out some gang of evil-hearted "abusers." It is how to structure tax planning frictions so as to minimize the resources wasted on avoiding taxes when they could be spent on improving the products and services underpinning the success of the American economy.

Background

The rise of corporate tax sheltering activity in recent years has grown increasingly hard to dispute. Even beyond the pervasive anecdotal evidence, including that contained in a devastating recent study by a Senate subcommittee on tax sheltering activity by the accounting firm KPMG,[4] there is compelling statistical evidence that increased gaps in recent years between companies' reported book income for accounting purposes and their reported taxable income reflect increased tax sheltering, in addition to increased accounting manipulations.[5] The reasons for the increase in tax sheltering activity are also easy to understand. Fundamentally, sheltering has become cheaper and spread by imitation, as more and more companies got away with it.

On the demand side, companies that were increasingly aggressive about managing, say, their inventory costs came to think of tax costs as no different and of their tax departments as in effect profit centers.[6] On the supply side, financial innovation increased the available tools for creative paper shuffling, and the rise of tax consulting work by the "Final Four" accounting firms (Deloitte Touche Tohmatsu, Ernst & Young, KPMG, and Price WaterhouseCoopers) may have mattered as well. When the big accounting firms began to get more involved in tax planning, they increased competitive pressures and brought a newly entrepreneurial spirit to the marketplace for tax services. Before, practitioners in the cozy legal world often served their own tax clients without aggressively soliciting new business or marketing their planning ideas widely. Leading firms' reputations had depended on being viewed as cautious and responsible rather than as creative or aggressive,[7] but increasingly, this has ceased to be good enough. Even temperamentally conservative law firms cannot wholly overlook the threat that, if they decline to endorse particular deals, their broader transaction work may migrate to rivals that are less scrupulous.

The Debate So Far

To date, most of the debate concerning corporate tax shelters, when not directed to the volume of activity or to whether it constitutes "abuse," has focused on whether the government should combat the shelters through black-letter rules or more open-ended standards.[8] A common illustration of the distinction between rules and standards, in the context of driving a car, is that a "standard" might require reasonable speed under all the circumstances, while a "rule" might specify a fifty-five mile-per-hour speed limit. Driving, of course, is governed by both rules and standards, because you can be ticketed even for driving within the speed limit if your speed is unreasonable under the circumstances (for example, because the road is icy).

To show how both standards and rules can apply to a given set of facts, consider the decision in *Compaq Computer Corp. v. Commissioner*.[9] In the transaction underlying this case, Compaq had prearranged a purchase and immediate resale of foreign stock. The idea was to be the owner of the stock at the precise moment when a dividend (subject to a foreign country's withholding tax) was paid, but then to sell the stock immediately, for a prearranged price. By doing this, Compaq hoped, in effect, to buy foreign tax credits, offsetting U.S. income tax liability, from foreign shareholders who could not have used the credits because they had no U.S. income tax liability to offset. The case was litigated under an economic substance standard. The Tax Court denied the credits on the ground that Compaq exhibited insufficient nontax business motivation and bore too little economic risk of ownership with respect to the stock. The Fifth Circuit then reversed the Tax Court, holding that the credits were allowable, based on what I argued was an egregious misreading of the facts.[10] The Fifth Circuit accepted, however, that Compaq was required to establish business purpose and economic substance for the credits to be allowed.

The use of a rule, instead of a standard, to address the same type of transaction is illustrated by section 901(k), which would apply today to a *Compaq*-style transaction but had not yet been enacted when the deal took place. Section 901(k) denies foreign tax credits to U.S. taxpayers that hold foreign stock unless the taxpayers hold the stock for less than fifteen days, counting only days when the taxpayer has not excessively hedged the economic risks associated with ownership. The provision thus imposes a blackletter legal requirement of economic substance (i.e., exposure to risks of ownership for a period that is not entirely trivial) that is likely to be relatively certain in its application to a given case, apart from the question of what constitutes excessive hedging.

The choice between rules and standards is indeed an important one. Among the key differences is that, since general standards already exist, they can apply to newly developed transactions without requiring an after-the-fact and purely prospective legislative or regulatory response. Rules such as section 901(k), by contrast, typically are enacted only after the government has learned about a particular new trick, by which time the inventors have probably moved on to newer tricks. A second difference is that, for good or ill, more loosely defined standards give the Internal Revenue Service greater discretion and flexibility in its responses. Rules make the tax code more predictable for tax planners, although whether this is good or bad, in cases where the planners are trying to skate as close as possible to the line separating permissible from impermissible transactions, has been debated at some length.

Despite the vigor of the rules versus standards debate, the similarities between the two as tools for combating corporate tax shelters are more important than the differences. Again, a rule such as section 901(k) is best seen as specifying the economic substance that is required for a *Compaq*-style transaction to work, rather than as departing from the idea of requiring economic substance. For this reason and because the reasons for (and against) requiring economic substance have been insufficiently explored in the literature, in this paper, I treat economic substance-style rules and standards mainly as interchangeable and examine the purposes served by both.

Responses by the Income Tax Law to Tax Sheltering

In general, the income tax law uses three types of tools to combat tax sheltering, or the deliberate creation of tax losses (or excess credits) to eliminate the tax liability on other income. The first tool is changing the substantive rules that the shelters exploit. If this were a matter of simple base broadening, then the path to eliminating tax shelters would be clear, even if politically difficult. Unfortunately, however, corporate tax shelters generally exploit structural rules within the income tax rather than tax preferences for particular industries. They typically take advantage of such features as the realization requirement, the distinction between debt and equity, and the rules permitting tax-free incorporation of a business or a set of assets. In general, these rules are too strongly embedded in the income tax for their elimination to be feasible (or even necessarily desirable) short of fundamental tax reform.

A second tool is the use of "schedular" rules that limit the types of income a particular deduction or credit is allowed to offset. For corporations as well as individuals, the use of capital losses[11] and foreign tax credits[12] is limited in this way. A number of additional schedular limitations, such as the passive loss rules[13] and investment interest limitation,[14] apply mainly to individuals and would be hard to extend to corporations without developing complicated rules for identifying separate lines of business activity. (This is easier to do for individuals, who typically have a primary job that can be distinguished from their investment activities.)

Schedular rules raise complicated efficiency issues of their own, which I discuss elsewhere.[15] Even if clearly desirable, however, they permit the taxpayer to reduce to zero the tax on a given category of income, restricting merely the use of losses or excess credits against other income. Thus, they fall short of ensuring that given categories of income will continue to be taxed, suggesting that, from the government's perspective, they require supplementation by other approaches.

The third tool is requiring economic substance, whether through rules or standards.[16] What does it mean to require economic substance? The term is not self-defining. Its meaning can change in different contexts and depends on how policymakers choose to interpret it. Nonetheless, its general import is easily conveyed. Transactions may be found to lack economic substance if they have little or no effect on the taxpayer's overall economic position. As an example, consider what Eugene Steuerle calls "pure tax arbitrages," such as simultaneously buying and selling the same asset.[17] Or a larger transaction may have economic effects but involve pointless extra steps that serve only to shoehorn it into a preferred category. To illustrate, consider *Waterman Steamship Corporation v. Commissioner*.[18] The taxpayer in this case sold a wholly owned subsidiary, potentially creating a taxable capital gain. Just before the sale, however, it created a large dividend payout obligation from the subsidiary (with suitable adjustment to the sale price), satisfied only after the sale through the use of cash infused into the subsidiary by the buyer. In this way, the corporation tried to transmute the taxable capital gain into tax-free dividends received. Unsuccessfully, as it turned out. The court held that the dividend payout would not have been engaged in but for the sale and had no purpose or effect other than reducing tax liability on the sale, and therefore was a sham.

Often, the assessment of economic substance turns critically on the taxpayer's risk position. Suppose a taxpayer wants to qualify as the tax owner of an asset, for example, so she can claim foreign tax credits or depreciation deductions. Even if she is the asset's legal owner, her ownership may be held to lack economic substance for tax purposes unless she can show that she bore some upside or downside economic risk with respect to the asset, rather than being completely insulated through side transactions with the same counterparties or others.

The Conundrum Posed by Economic Substance Requirements

Support for an economic substance approach involves a conundrum that has been little noticed in the literature. Compaq, for example, indisputably could have enjoyed the tax benefit it sought from effectively purchasing foreign tax credits had it been willing to take greater economic risks with respect to the foreign stock that it used in the transaction. An economic substance approach thereby creates a tax incentive to bear such risks of ownership instead of not bearing them. Yet, it is hard to see any direct policy reason why the tax authorities should want to influence risk-bearing decisions by a taxpayer such as Compaq.[19]

In illustration, suppose that the sole effect of section 901(k) was to induce all companies interested in cross-border dividend stripping to hold the stock for sixteen days rather than (like Compaq) one hour. That is, suppose no prospective shelterers were deterred by the holding period even though they did not really want the stock they were momentarily holding in order to claim foreign tax credits. The result would be to burden these purchasers without providing any fiscal benefit to the Treasury or otherwise improving in any way the efficiency or distributional effects of the income tax. The same number of transactions, with the same revenue cost to the Treasury, would be going on as before. The only difference would be that the companies would face a period of undesired economic risk (or costly adjustment to avoid the risk) until they were free to dump the stock, without this burden implying offsetting benefit to anyone else.[20]

However, the preceding scenario is not entirely realistic. Suppose, alternatively, that the fifteen-day holding period deterred all *Compaq*-style transactions, without affecting any economically based decisions to purchase, hold, or sell foreign stock. Now section

901(k) might seem unambiguously beneficial. It would not actually induce any undesired risk bearing, and it would eliminate an entire class of transactions aimed purely at importing foreign tax credits to the U.S. system.

So, the rationale for an economic substance approach is that it may generate frictional impediments to certain socially undesirable tax planning. One could dramatize this rationale by thinking of taxpayers as metaphorically headed downstream with a foot on each of two rafts: the economic planning raft and the tax planning raft. Each taxpayer aims to end up with the best economic results and the best tax results. Absent an economic substance approach, he can in effect lash the two rafts tightly together, steer the best route from an economic standpoint, and end up with the preferred tax result. Under an economic substance approach, however, the two rafts may drift sufficiently far apart that the taxpayer is forced to jump off one raft, letting it drift away while he stands entirely on the other. If he jumps off the economic planning raft to stay on the tax planning raft, then all the approach has done is send him to an economic destination some distance from where he wanted to go. But if he jumps off the tax planning raft, then the approach has succeeded. He gets where he wanted economically but no longer enjoys the best tax results.

The desirability of an economic substance approach depends on two main things. The first is the social value of deterring a given transaction. The second is the extent to which the approach succeeds in creating such deterrence. In other words, how often does it actually deter the transactions, as opposed to merely inducing taxpayers to jump through a few extra hoops before getting the desired tax consequences anyway?

From this perspective, economic substance is just a tool for accomplishing aims that have little to do with how one might define it as a matter of internal logic. Leaving aside the institutional reasons why (for courts, in particular) economic substance might be an especially useful tool, one could just as well condition favorable tax consequences on whether the taxpayer's chief financial officer can execute twenty back-somersaults in the IRS National Office on midnight of April Fool's Day, if such a requirement turns out to achieve a better ratio of deterrence to wasteful effort in meeting requirements that are pointless in themselves.

Pervasiveness of This Type of Trade-Off in the Existing Income Tax

Trade-offs such as those posed by an economic substance requirement may seem perverse, but they are pervasive in the income tax law. Consider just a few examples, such as the at-risk rules[21] and passive loss rules[22] for individuals, which burden tax sheltering through a risk requirement in the former case and a material participation requirement in the latter. Or consider the wash sale rules,[23] which deny loss recognition on the sale of stock or securities if the taxpayer buys an identical asset within thirty days. All these rules mean that individuals have to accept certain undesired consequences that benefit no one else as the price of receiving a tax break.

In some circumstances, imposing otherwise pointless frictions on tax strategies may raise efficiency. The realization requirement offers an illustration. Suppose there are two classes of assets: those that have no taxable gain or loss until they are sold and those that are taxed on a current accrual basis. The former assets would be tax-favored by deferral (assuming their return is on average positive). And strategic trading, the practice of indefinitely holding "winners" and immediately selling "losers," makes the tax bias in favor of these assets considerably greater. It even holds out the prospect of infinite loss deductions. Taxpayers can choose whether or not to realize their gains and losses, and this choice is completely unconstrained if it need have no economic consequences, such as by requiring a change in the taxpayer's overall risk position. Requiring economic substance raises the cost of that choice and thereby reduces the tax bias in favor of realization assets. It is an empirical question what exercise price for the strategic trading option causes the least waste, but there is no reason to assume that the socially optimal exercise price generally is zero (as in the case of a pure election to treat all losses and no gains as realized).

Identifying Corporate Tax Shelters

While there is no Platonic definition of a corporate tax shelter and commentators may disagree about describing them in general and identifying them in particular cases, the core idea is related to economic substance. Generally, a corporate tax shelter is a carefully tailored transaction that exploits various tax rules in what are likely to be unintended ways, to obtain favorable tax results without significantly affecting the taxpayer's economic position.[24] Or, to put it more colloquially, it is a corporate transaction involving energetic paper shuffling aimed at having favorable tax consequences along with no, or next to no, economic consequences other than the tax consequences.[25]

Typically, the transactions involve some sort of a United States income tax arbitrage.[26] That is, if X is the taxpayer investing in a corporate transaction, then for each dollar that goes from X to counterparty Y, an offsetting dollar (leaving aside the fees X pays) goes from Y back to X, but the tax treatment of the offsetting dollars is asymmetric. X's tax benefit from taking account of the dollar it "loses" exceeds its tax detriment from taking account of the dollar it "gains." Thus, X is an aftertax winner while Y, for one reason or another (such as not being a U.S. taxpayer), does not commensurately lose.

The following three examples may help flesh out this idea and show how corporate tax shelters typically exploit structural rules within the income tax, rather than tax preferences for particular industries. I make no effort to be cutting-edge in these examples, since only those practicing the black arts can really hope to be so (and they are not talking). Newer transactions resemble the old even if they exploit distinctive provisions of the income tax law in novel ways.

Example 1: Cross-Border Dividend-Stripping. This is the trans-action underlying the *Compaq* case and apparently put to bed by the enactment of section 901(k), with its fifteen-day holding period for foreign stock. It arbitrages the foreign tax credit, each allowable dollar of which reduces one's U.S. tax liability by a full dollar, against the inclusion of extra taxable income, each dollar of which increases a U.S. company's tax liability but only by the marginal tax rate, which tops out for corporations at 35 percent.

To illustrate this transaction, suppose that foreign company A's stock trades for $100 per share, and that A declares a dividend of $10 per share to be paid on a specified date in the near future. However, the country in which A is incorporated subjects the dividends to a 30 percent withholding tax, meaning that even a tax-exempt holder gets only $7 per share when the dividend is paid. Assume further that market evidence suggests that, if A's stock is trading for $100 per share just before a dividend of $10 per share is paid, it is likely to trade for $93 per share immedi-ately afterward.[27]

American company B buys stock of company A for $100 just before the dividend is paid and sells the stock for $93 just after-ward. For each such share, therefore, B pays tax on $10 of dividend income, deducts a $7 capital loss (summing to a net income inclusion of $3), and claims $3 of foreign tax credits. At a 35 per-cent marginal tax rate, the $3 of added net income increases B's tax liability by $1.05, but this still leaves B $1.95 ahead after claiming $3 worth of foreign tax credits.

One problem with the transaction as just described is that it may involve some risk that the price of A's stock will change in an unanticipated fashion during B's brief moment of ownership. Indeed, if B relied on open market transactions, the very fact that it was buying a lot of A stock at one moment and then selling it all a moment later might change the stock price to B's disad-vantage. Accordingly, in actual transactions such as *Compaq*, the stock purchases and sales, price and all, were completely pre-arranged, permitting the taxpayer to be 100 percent certain of breaking even apart from the transaction fee and the anticipated tax savings.

Suppose that Congress had expressly blessed such transactions, rather than belatedly impeding them through the enactment of section 901(k). What would be the broader result? So long as enough foreign stock was out there with prices that responded like the A stock to the payment of dividends subject to withholding, the consequence would presumably be that no well-advised U.S. company with sufficient capital gains (needed to use the $7 capital loss in the example) would have to pay U.S. tax on foreign source passive income, which is the only type of income against which the foreign tax credits could be used. If not for the schedular rules so limiting the use of capital losses and foreign tax credits, the result would be the elimination of all U.S. taxes on U.S. companies' foreign source income, if—perhaps a big if—enough foreign stock was out there that changed price ex dividend like that of A.[28] The resulting exemption of certain foreign source income would come at the social price of transaction costs associated with arranging the purchase and immediate resale of large quantities of foreign stock.

Example 2: High-Basis, Low-Value Shelter. A second illustrative corporate tax shelter transaction appeared no later than the mid-1990s and, as of early 2004, may still have been around (although anyone engaging in it was not broadcasting this fact). Here, the tax arbitrage involved creating an economic loss and precisely offsetting economic gain overseas, then arranging for the loss to be "imported" to the United States income tax system and thus deducted, while the gain stayed overseas.

To illustrate, suppose that C, a foreign accommodation party, creates a currency straddle, for example, by "betting" through derivative financial instruments both that the dollar will rise against the euro and that the euro will rise against the dollar. (This is likely to be done in a jurisdiction where currency straddles have no tax consequences.) Each leg of the straddle costs C $100 to acquire, and at the end, depending on how the dollar performs against the euro in the interim, one leg is worth $170 while the other is worth $30. C contributes the losing leg of the straddle to a newly created subsidiary of D, a United States company, in exchange for stock of the new subsidiary, in a tax-free incorporation transaction.[29] D contributes cash to the subsidiary in exchange for the rest of the stock. The subsidiary then redeems C's stock for $30, which is the value of the straddle leg that C contributed, plus whatever fee C can command for agreeing to participate in the transaction.

D ends up with a subsidiary that possesses an asset (the losing leg of the straddle) that has a built-in $70 tax loss (the difference between its $30 value and the $100 basis that was carried over from its cost basis in the hands of C). This built-in loss can be realized at any time. Since losses on foreign currency transactions are ordinary rather than capital,[30] no schedular rules would limit its use to eliminate U.S. income tax liability.

In consequence, if the Treasury unconditionally blessed this transaction, it could be used with the greatest of ease to eliminate all United States income tax liability of all companies that had (or could hire) the expertise to arrange it. The creation of foreign currency losses, unlike the acquisition of foreign stock that behaves ex dividend like that in example 1, is not limited by market forces of supply and demand. After all, each currency loss in the transaction is part of an arbitrage that nets to zero. Similarly, suppose that, when you bet on coin tosses, you were allowed to deduct all losses while excluding all gains. You could then create unlimited losses if you liked. You would not need to have good credit, money in the bank, or strong nerves to bet, say, $100 billion with the same counterparty both that a given coin toss will come out heads and that it will come out tails. No matter how the coin toss came out, your "loss" would be perfectly hedged and secured by your "gain."

The reason why, despite this transaction, there still is a U.S. corporate income tax is that, at least when it is done in the pure form just described, it clearly runs afoul of the common law doctrine requiring that tax-effective transactions must have economic substance and serve nontax business purposes.[31] But some taxpayers may have persuaded themselves that, by minimally tweaking the transaction to give it some appearance of colorable economic substance, they could at least treat it as offering a nonfraudulent reporting position.

Example 3: Sale-Leaseback with or without Financing. Tax-motivated sale-leasebacks have been around for many decades, but they remain popular among taxpayers and are a current source of concern to the U.S. Treasury. The usual idea behind them is to transfer tax ownership of an asset from one person to another, thus permitting the transferee rather than the transferor to claim depreciation deductions with respect to the asset, simply by arranging a set of circular cash flows between them. The underlying motivation is that the transferor cannot use the U.S. depreciation deductions, because it is either foreign, a tax-exempt entity, or a U.S. company with substantial net operating losses.

Sale-leasebacks and related transactions have evolved over the years to take a variety of forms and use extra complicating features such as back-to-back leases (where a given taxpayer simultaneously becomes both a lessor and a lessee of the same property). However, a couple of basic variations on a greatly simplified transaction can be used to illustrate the core idea. Suppose that Congress allows favorable depreciation for a given type of asset, perhaps with the aim of stimulating investment therein. Or consider that U.S. companies can deduct depreciation on buildings (like other business property) they own through European branches, whereas European municipal governments, not being U.S. taxpayers, obviously get no such deduction for their buildings.

Party E owns an asset, worth $100 million, depreciable over ten years for U.S. tax purposes. However, E effectively cannot deduct this depreciation in the United States, whether because it is a U.S. company with net operating losses (meaning that the deduction is allowed but has no value) or because it is a European municipal government with an office building that it uses as a town hall. Company F pays a lot of U.S. income tax and could use the depreciation on E's asset, but it has absolutely no desire actually to bear the economics of any such asset. E purports to sell the asset to F for $100 million. Of this amount, F pays E only $5 million in cash. F borrows the remaining $95 million from E and agrees to pay interest on this loan of $8 million per year. Meanwhile, since E remains the party that actually wants to use the asset, the parties simultaneously agree that E will rent it from F for $8 million per year. As a result, there is no net cash flow between the parties other than the initial $5 million that goes from F to E.

After ten years, when the asset has been depreciated to zero, the $95 million loan becomes due and the lease expires. At this time, however, E has a call option entitling it to buy the asset from F for $95 million, and F has a put option entitling it to sell the asset to E for $95 million. One way or another, therefore, E ends up repurchasing the asset in exchange for cancellation of F's $95 million debt. Accordingly, there is no further net cash flow between the parties, even when the transaction unwinds and E's legal ownership is restored. F has simply paid E $5 million up front in exchange for the right to deduct $100 million over ten years.[32]

In an alternative version of this transaction, E actually wants to borrow $100 million in cash. F, a lender, pays E this amount for legal title to the asset, which F immediately leases back to E. For each of the next ten years, E pays F $8 million that, due to the transaction's form as a sale, is denominated rent, rather than interest. At the end of the ten years, put and call options ensure that E buys the asset back from F for $100 million (effectively repaying the loan). But F gets the depreciation deductions during the interim and presumably compensates E through the interest rate.

In this "financing" version of the sale-leaseback transaction, just as in the *Waterman Steamship* case mentioned previously, something of a business character, rather than a purely tax character, has indeed happened. E actually got $100 million from F, then repaid the money after ten years, after paying $8 million annually in the interim. Only, one might be inclined to think that this was really a loan, misleadingly structured as a sale and repurchase through the creation of offsetting and otherwise pointless extra steps so that F, rather than E, gets to claim ten years of depreciation deductions. To say that nothing happened here but paper shuffling requires defining the relevant "transaction," serving no purposes beyond tax minimization, as the extra steps that took place apart from simply arranging a loan. This exercise of bifurcating the overall transaction into its real and purely tax-motivated components might beg the question of how we define "real" transactions. But, if one does not engage in the exercise, tax shelter transactions become easy to legitimate by the simple course of "stapling" them to other, more substantial transactions that might have taken place in any event.

These sale-leaseback transactions, because they have been simplified for ease of exposition, might not be respected for tax purposes under existing law. Well-established rules require greater indicia of economic substance,[33] designed to ensure that the tax owner puts in more cash and bears at least some small component of the risks we might consider associated with economic ownership. Yet, the currently required level of economic substance for sale-leasebacks is so slight that practitioner David Hariton calls the permitted transactions "silly leasing."[34] Recent efforts by the IRS to crack down on sale-leasebacks, or on the related "lease-in, lease-out" (LILO) transactions, have been impeded by both the difficulty of drawing workable lines and protaxpayer precedents in the case law and IRS ruling history.

What would be the effect of allowing all sale-leasebacks and LILOs to be tax effective, with no economic substance requirement whatsoever?[35] With respect to depreciable property in the United States, incentives to invest in property that gets preferential depreciation would be strengthened, because the deductions would never be "wasted" by going to persons that cannot use them. Whether this would be a good or bad thing depends on what one thinks of Congress as an economic policymaker when it creates a nonlevel playing field through its varyingly preferential depreciation rules. There also would be more sale-leasebacks and LILOs, resulting in more paper-shuffling transactions but perhaps a lower social cost per transaction. And there would be less (i.e., no) tax-motivated distortion of the economics of lease arrangements in response to the incentive to optimize tax ownership, which now would be purely elective.

One thing that would *not* happen, as a consequence of permitting unlimited sale-leasebacks with respect to property located in the United States, is the elimination of the corporate income tax. The built-in limit, which was absent in the case of high-basis, low-value shelters, is the need for someone to invest in the assets being depreciated. As the enhanced tax incentive from ensuring that the deductions are never wasted increases investment in the assets, their pretax return is bid down, leading to a stable equilibrium resembling that if the tax preference had simply been nominally more generous rather than more readily transferable.

This relatively benign conclusion may not hold, however, for the use of sale-leasebacks to import to the U.S. tax system depreciation deductions that relate to foreign property, such as the European municipalities' town halls. If any asset in the world can be converted into a U.S. asset for purposes of U.S. tax depreciation, simply through paper shuffling and the arrangement of reciprocal cash flows, then the entire U.S. tax base is potentially at risk.

Evaluating Corporate Tax Shelters and an Economic Substance Approach

The discussion thus far, although admittedly sketchy relative to the issues and the diversity of potential transactions, nonetheless points to a number of important conclusions regarding corporate tax shelters and the use of an economic substance approach to discourage them. Key conclusions include the following.

1. Limited or unlimited? It depends and is hard to tell. Some corporate tax shelter transactions are limited in potential volume and the amount of corporate tax revenue that they can be used to offset, but others are not so limited. Two main issues determine the degree to which a transaction's volume and revenue consequences are limited. The first is whether it requires the use of an actual (and not just a financial) asset, such as depreciable equipment, that inevitably is limited in supply. The second is whether the tax law uses schedular rules to limit the deductions and credits the transaction would generate. Whether a given transaction is thus limited can be hard to judge without a broader empirical inquiry. For example, sale-leasebacks may seem to be limited if one focuses only on transactions involving tangible property located in the United States. But the limits may disappear if depreciation deductions can be imported from abroad. In the case of a transaction (such as that in *Compaq*) that involves generating capital losses, which generally are allowable only against capital gains, a key consideration may be how readily taxpayers can make the losses usable by converting ordinary income into capital gains.

2. Corporate tax shelters are not defensible as a shortcut to corporate integration or the enactment of a consumption tax. Transactions that are potentially unlimited in their capacity to eliminate companies' tax liability should be considered dangerous and destructive, even if one dislikes the corporate income tax, and whether any such dislike is founded on favoring corporate integration or preferring consumption taxation to income taxation. Eliminating the corporate-level tax might be desirable, although preferably without all of the paper shuffling that the shelter transactions entail, if corporate income were being taxed directly to shareholders. But this is not happening. Earnings that remain in corporate solution need not be taxed to individuals at any particular time. For example, if a shareholder dies before receiving corporate distributions, her stock basis is increased to fair market value, and selling the stock back to the company would extract her share of the earnings from corporate solution with no capital gain. Even when companies pay dividends, the marginal tax rate on their recipients is generally only 15 percent.

Likewise, while it might be desirable to convert the corporate income tax into a consumption tax, this is not what corporate tax shelter transactions do. The corporate-level tax base would be consumption, rather than income, if business outlays generally were expensed, rather than being capitalized as many of them must be under an income tax. But allowing companies to deduct or credit supposed expenses they do not really incur economically (such as due to an offsetting receipt) has nothing whatsoever to do with shifting from income tax to consumption tax accounting.

3. *There is a potential rationale for corporate tax shelter transactions that are sufficiently limited, but no particular reason to think that this rationale will often apply.* When schedular rules or a limited supply of a given asset sufficiently limit a particular corporate tax shelter transaction, it is possible that allowing the transaction to work for tax purposes, without regard to economic substance requirements, has beneficial consequences on balance. Consider sale-leasebacks involving a type of equipment that Congress intends to encourage through favorable depreciation rules. If Congress's decision to favor this asset is good economic policy, an economic substance approach that limits sale-leasebacks simply gets in the way. Even if Congress's decision is bad economic policy, allowing sale-leasebacks is likely to be better than inducing Congress to overcome the lost taxpayer responsiveness by making the nominal tax preference even larger. While either approach can match the other in the level of investment in the tax-favored asset it induces, the approach of more liberally allowing sale-leasebacks may reduce taxpayers' socially undesirable incentive to establish economic substance by distorting the economic ownership of the assets relative to what would be desirable in the absence of any such requirement.

Likewise, suppose a given transaction permits taxpayers to wipe out their U.S. income tax liability in a given foreign income "basket" (as in *Compaq*, if the transaction were still permitted and did not require that the taxpayer have capital gains, also assuming a sufficient supply of suitable foreign stock). Various commentators have argued for the adoption of a territorial system, in which the United States would no longer tax at least specified categories of outbound investment by U.S. taxpayers.[36] While these proposals relate mainly to active business income, as opposed to passive or portfolio investment like that which the taxpayer sheltered in *Compaq*, one can certainly imagine the possibility that a given transaction would enable companies to achieve a socially desirable narrowing of the outbound tax base (albeit through self-help that required potentially costly paper shuffling). But there is no particular reason to think that corporate tax shelter transactions generally tend in such an innocuous direction. They are driven by the available sheltering technologies, not by policy considerations of which sectors are overtaxed.

4. Economic substance requirements that require the acceptance of some economic risk as the price of receiving a tax benefit can be surprisingly effective. One puzzle posed by economic substance requirements is why they are as effective as anecdotal evidence strongly suggests. In illustration, consider *Compaq*-style transactions and the requirement of section 901(k) that one hold the foreign company's stock, bearing the risk of value changes, for at least fifteen days to be allowed to use the foreign tax credits. For the shareholders of a company such as Compaq, there is no particular reason to mind if the company bears such a risk with respect to another company's stock. After all, the shareholders ought, as a matter of prudent investment strategy, to have internationally diversified portfolios in any event. In earlier writing about corporate tax shelters, I suggest that the rule's effectiveness depends on an agency cost from the shareholders' perspective.[37] The officers of a publicly traded U.S. corporation may be reluctant to counsel the taking of economic risks that lie outside the scope of their company's business in connection with tax planning, based on the view that they, as individuals, have more to lose reputationally if the risks go sour than they have to gain if things turn out positively. In anecdotal support of this view from my own personal experience, practitioners engaged in giving tax advice to publicly traded companies frequently mention the tax officers' extreme reluctance to accept nontax economic risk as a part of tax deals, even if the companies take substantial economic risks in their business planning.

5. *Economic substance requirements should be evaluated in terms of their effectiveness in deterring undesirable transactions relative to the transaction and other costs they end up increasing not based on their supposed internal logic.* Economic substance requirements are often defended based on some intuitive notion that they are inherently logically or morally right. In the case of sale-leasebacks, for example, it might be argued that only the true owner ought to be allowed to deduct the depreciation. Permitting the owner in effect to sell the deductions to someone else without truly selling the underlying asset (the extreme case of separating tax ownership from economic ownership) ostensibly offends some underlying notion of logic or equity.

Such a claim cannot be assessed without asking what the tax system's goals ought to be. A commonly accepted position would be at least partly consequentialist, or concerned with selecting tax (and other government) rules that have good economic and social effects, generally relating to efficiency and wealth distribution. If one accepts this very basic point, one needs to ask why there should be any reluctance to let one person sell tax attributes to another person, and the answer can only be that it would have bad consequences, presumably to other taxpayers, since the parties to the transaction must think that it benefits them. And once the issue has been put this way, we are right in the mode of analysis that this paper suggests, concerning, for example, effects on the economic policies that Congress might be rightly or wrongly pursuing when it enacts depreciation rules for various assets.

The argument in this paper for deterring deduction sales by requiring accompanying economic substance that the parties may find inconvenient is therefore entirely pragmatic; hence, my earlier comment that one could just as well condition favorable tax consequences on whether the taxpayer's chief financial officer can execute twenty back-somersaults in the IRS National Office on midnight of April Fool's Day, if such a requirement turned out to achieve a better ratio of deterrence to wasteful effort in meeting requirements that are pointless in themselves. How much substance should be required is an empirical question that depends on such considerations as the desirability of deterring the transactions at issue and the ratio at different levels of required substance between successful deterrence and inducing additional waste.

6. *Both rules and standards should be used in requiring economic substance.* Neither rules nor standards alone can ensure that an adequate level of economic substance is required of tax-significant transactions. One key reason for using a standard is that the IRS and the courts can apply it across the board, without raising issues of undue retroactivity, even if the government failed to anticipate a particular trick and state in advance that it does not work. There are simply too many fault lines in the existing income tax and too many clever people laboring behind closed doors to find new ways to exploit these fault lines for after-the-fact prospective responses to be adequate. However, once a given transaction or fault line comes to Congress's attention, it may make good sense to craft a blackletter rule that unambiguously requires a particular type of economic substance. Again, the fifteen-day requirement of section 901(k) provides a useful illustration.

7. *Aggressive corporate tax sheltering, like aggressive accounting manipulations, can lead to a dangerous collapse of broader social norms.* A final issue concerns the relationship between the rise over the last decade of corporate tax sheltering and the simultaneous rise of financial accounting manipulation. Plainly, the two phenomena have a lot in common. They are similarly market driven, both on the demand side, by increased performance pressures on corporate

management, and on the supply side, by the rise of entrepreneurialism and competition in the formerly cozy and secluded legal and accounting professions. They share the same spirit and use many of the same tools, such as "special purpose entities" and complicated financial instruments.

One difference between the two, underlying my own sense that the word *abuse* is not really helpful or enlightening in the corporate tax shelter area, lies in the different nature of the financial accounting and tax reporting enterprises. Financial accounting is not supposed to be an adversarial system, with the management on one side and the shareholders on the other. Rather, the management is supposed to serve the shareholders' interests by reporting income accurately. When we recognize the inevitable divergences in interest between the managers and the shareholders, we call this a problem of agency cost rather than hoping to balance the managers' interests against those of the shareholders (which can be handled through arm's length compensation agreements).

With respect to companies' tax reporting, the duties are more complicated. Managers serve the shareholders' interests when they seek to lower the company's tax liability, and from the standpoint of the shareholders' economic self-interest, it does not matter whether they use fair means or foul, unless they unduly blunder into a penalty situation. Moreover, to a degree, we think of the tax system as adversarial in character and taxpayers as entitled to take reasonable reporting positions that are in their self-interest, as opposed to being expected to attempt a completely neutral and objective application of the tax law to their economic affairs.

But tax compliance is meant to be adversarial only to a degree. The tax system cannot function properly if taxpayers, rather than regarding compliance with the law as a duty, start regarding cheating under the threat of penalty as simply a risky investment, like buying the stock of a speculative startup. Norms of compliance and trust, based on the idea that we are all better off if we behave honorably so that the system can function, are therefore critical.

As a societal coordination problem, tax compliance has the structure of a prisoner's dilemma. If you can get away with cheating, it always makes you (financially) better off, but we are all better off collectively if we all agree to comply rather than cheat. Adversarial attitudes can be disastrous in the context of a prisoner's dilemma, because (if people cannot observe each other) it means that everyone cheats.

Aggressive paper shuffling to minimize tax liability is not identical to cheating if its being impermissible under the existing state of the law is not clear-cut. But there is an issue of degree here, and a slippery slope. Taking self-interested but reasonable reporting positions slides over into taking positions that are more and more unlikely to be sustained and, therefore, deliberately kept secret, converting the entire enterprise into one of playing the "audit lottery" rather than taking a position that one believes is actually reasonable under the law. At a certain point, although it is hard to say exactly where, aggressive planning merges into outright cheating. Even before that point is reached, the former starts to have many of the same bad effects on general compliance as the latter.

The difference between corporate tax sheltering and financial accounting manipulation narrows once we recognize the nonadversarial and cooperative element of tax compliance. Just as the managers should act in the interest of the shareholders when they file accounting statements, so the management and shareholders should act in the interest of taxpayers generally by confining their pursuit of self-interest in tax minimization to strategies and reporting positions that are reasonably within the spirit of the law. In each case, there is a risk of system breakdown if deception spreads sufficiently to become the new norm. So, dramatic responses may be needed in both to restore public trust and cooperation.

Conclusion

Are corporations abusing the tax system? Attempting to minimize tax liability is not inherently an abuse, unless it involves violating existing law. To a degree, corporate tax advisors fail to serve their clients and managers fail to advance the interests of shareholders if they do not consider tax minimization strategies. But aggressive tax sheltering that crosses or even nears the boundaries of what is legally permitted can have negative effects on broader social norms of tax compliance.

Such issues would not be raised by corporate tax shelters that lack economic substance if there were no reason to require such substance. But such a requirement is necessary to limit taxpayers' increasing efforts to exploit arbitrage opportunities that could otherwise be used to exempt large categories of corporate income from bearing any tax, while running up transaction costs. Tax sheltering opportunities are likely to continue being discovered by taxpayers on a regular basis and detected by the government only later, if at all. It appears clear, moreover, at least at present, that one can significantly discourage these transactions by requiring the taxpayers who would engage in them to accept at least a modicum of accompanying business risk. The government, therefore, ought to continue (and perhaps expand) applying a general economic substance standard, along with narrower black-letter rules that specify what substance is required in particular settings. Only fundamental tax reform—if even that—is likely to make an economic substance approach unnecessary.

2

More Revenues, Less Distortion?
Responding to Cross-Border Tax Arbitrage

Introduction

Twenty years ago, "foreign tax" (the prevailing label for U.S. taxation of inbound and outbound investment) was merely a niche specialty in tax practice, like giving companies tax advice about their pension plans. Today, if it is still a niche specialty, then so is giving tax advice to corporations. The growth of "foreign tax" practice reflects the rise, not only of multinational business enterprises, but worldwide capital market integration. Suppose a prominent company wants to raise capital. Whether its place of incorporation, its business activities, and its current owners are all American, all foreign, or some mix of the two, it may want to consider tapping both American and foreign investors. This may require sophisticated "foreign tax" advice from American tax lawyers regarding optimal structuring methods for companies and investors, whether funds would flow into the United States or out of it.

The growth of cross-border business enterprises and capital market integration increased taxpayers' experience of both the hazards and the opportunities associated with cross-border tax planning. On the hazards side, countries may slant their "sourcing"

This chapter is adapted from an earlier article that appeared in the *Chicago Journal of International Law.* See Daniel N. Shaviro, "Money on the Table? Responding to Cross-Border Tax Arbitrage," *Chicago Journal of International Law* 3 (2002): 317–31.

rules for income measurement (used to distinguish domestic- from foreign-source income) with an eye to collectively taxing more than 100 percent of a given multinational's profits. But the opportunities side is enriched by the fact that taxpayers, when not constrained by business necessity, are in the position of making the first move. All the different national legal regimes and sets of rules within a given regime may give taxpayers a rich set of options regarding, not only what to do, but how they want to characterize, for tax law purposes, whatever they do.

The last twenty years have seen increased harvesting of profitable cross-border opportunities, not just in business and portfolio investment, but also in tax planning. The "corporate tax shelter" phenomenon I discuss elsewhere in this volume[1] sometimes involves using foreigners to aid predominantly United States–directed planning. For example, foreigners may serve as tax-indifferent accommodation parties to whom the U.S. tax rules notionally (but irrelevantly) assign "phantom income" that matches the "phantom losses" directed to U.S. taxpayers.

A second, very different scenario involves tax planning that it is hard to call predominantly directed either at the United States or other foreign tax systems. Rather, like torts in the famous view of Ronald Coase (where neither the railway nor the hayfield would have produced a fire unless they were right next to each other),[2] this tax planning involves the contiguity of two individually unremarkable but ill-matched results to achieve an overall worldwide tax result that potentially is remarkable. Many of the transactions having this character are commonly known as *cross-border tax arbitrages*. As we will see, while these transactions are defined semantically, they tend to have certain essential traits in common that facilitate thinking about them as a coherent category.

During the Clinton administration, the United States Treasury proposed to deny U.S. tax benefits to taxpayers engaging in certain of these transactions. Vehement opposition forced the Treasury to back off somewhat but without renouncing its concerns.[3] Under the George W. Bush administration, the Treasury Department has seemed generally less eager to proceed in this area, but it has not abandoned the struggle and indeed in some instances continued to wage the same or similar fights.[4]

Unfortunately, the debate about cross-border tax arbitrage too often failed to focus adequately on relevant tax policy considerations, which relate in particular to the public economics concepts of "national welfare," or efficiency from the U.S. standpoint, and "worldwide welfare," or efficiency from a global standpoint.[5] The U.S. Treasury Department has not fully explained why it is concerned about taxpayers' favorable worldwide tax results if the U.S. tax results, standing alone, would have been unobjectionable. Commentators sometimes misconstrue the Treasury's policy concern as based either on the belief that "we . . . have a monopoly on correctness"[6] or on a perverse preoccupation with other countries' totally separate tax affairs. "Why [in responding to certain U.S.-German rental deals arranged by clever taxpayers] . . . should we be concerned about the rate of tax they are called upon to pay on rental income in Berlin?"[7] Under this view, however, it is hard to see why we would care enough about double taxation to respond to it by offering foreign tax credits.

This paper therefore briefly examines cross-border tax arbitrage in light of national and worldwide welfare considerations, along with an additional point, the importance of countries' strategic interactions, which are directly raised in this setting. It concludes that the transactions, while not really arbitrages or tax arbitrages as these terms are commonly used, can have troubling efficiency consequences. Accordingly, where duplicative tax benefits are being achieved in each of two countries, either country, by unilaterally denying its benefit, may combine raising revenue with increasing both national and worldwide efficiency. The only problem is that the other country may want to share in the revenue gain from allowing the tax benefits, potentially leading to double denial of any tax benefit. While this is probably not as bad a result as duplicative allowance of tax benefits, since taxpayers can use self-help to minimize the resulting problems, it suggests that bilateral coordination to allow the tax benefits a total of only once may be the best response when feasible. This would require greater coordination between countries' tax systems than has been usual to date, but it does not require anything approaching worldwide harmonization of tax systems. Countries need not adopt the same rules to cooperate in addressing peculiar interactions between their rules.

What Is Cross-Border Tax Arbitrage?

Cross-border tax arbitrage has been defined as taking advantage of inconsistencies between different countries' tax rules to achieve a more favorable result than that which would have resulted from investing in a single jurisdiction.[8] Without delving too deeply into technical minutiae, two relatively simple examples may help those who are not tax specialists grasp the underlying idea.

Dual Resident Companies. Countries typically apply residence taxation, not just to individuals who are citizens or live inside their borders, but also to certain legal entities such as corporations. Yet, the residence of a corporation often is not obvious or self-defining (leaving aside the question of why it should matter to begin with). Suppose, for example, a company is incorporated in country A; has its main headquarters in country B; operates factories in countries C, D, and E; and sells its products through sales outlets that it maintains in all these countries plus twenty more. Where is it resident? The United States bases the determination of corporate residence on where a given company is incorporated. The United Kingdom, by contrast, is among the countries that treat a company as a resident if it is deemed to be locally managed and controlled. A corporation can therefore qualify as both a U.S. and a U.K. resident, if it is incorporated here but managed and controlled (at least for U.K. tax purposes) there.

One further important detail is that, in both the United States and the United Kingdom, a group of commonly owned domestic corporations can file a consolidated return, resulting for some purposes in treatment of the group as if it were a single corporate taxpayer.[9] Thus, one member's losses can be deducted against another's income. Fertile minds soon realized that this jointly followed rule, in combination with the disparity between the two countries' corporate residence rules, could be exploited to the taxpayer's advantage.

Suppose a multinational enterprise incorporates a company in the United States and places this company's headquarters in the United Kingdom, thus making it a dual resident company (DRC) that both countries treat as a "native." The DRC can be consolidated both with the enterprise's U.K. corporations in the United Kingdom and with its U.S. corporations in the United States. Suppose further that both consolidated groups have positive taxable income but the DRC incurs tax losses. (This can be arranged through such means as making it highly leveraged and manipulating the reported "transfer prices" on its transactions with other group members.) If otherwise permitted by both countries, the DRC's tax losses can be deducted twice, against the income of both the U.K. and U.S. groups. The result of this double deduction is that an amount of the overall worldwide group's income equal to the DRC's loss is taxed nowhere.

The United States responded to this gambit in 1986 by enacting a rule that denied the use of DRC losses on consolidated returns.[10] Some years later, the United Kingdom followed suit with a similar rule (although several other countries that apply a headquarters rule for corporate residence rule have not done so).[11] At present, therefore, the tax losses of DRCs are allowable against consolidated group income in neither the United States nor the United Kingdom.

Double-Dip Leases. A similar tax planning idea takes advantage of disparities between countries' rules for determining who gets depreciation deductions. Suppose that legal title to an airplane is held by a French taxpayer, but beneficial economic ownership goes to an American taxpayer under a long-term lease. France and the United States agree that depreciation deductions go only to the owner of the property, as defined for tax purposes. However, France bases tax ownership exclusively on legal title, while

United States tax law sometimes relies on indicia of economic ownership.

Therefore, with careful planning, the airplane's acquisition cost may end up being deducted in full by both the legal owner in France and the beneficial owner in the United States. This may result in up-front worldwide nontaxation of an amount equal to the acquisition cost. Despite the similarity to the result of creating a DRC with tax losses, double-dip leases, while widely noted, have not been challenged even by the (at times assertive) United States Treasury.

Other Cross-Border Tax Arbitrages. In recent years, perhaps the most fertile source of similar transactions has been the so-called check-the-box regulations that the U.S. Treasury issued in December 1996. These regulations permit taxpayers straightforwardly to elect, for U.S. tax purposes, whether certain legal entities should be regarded as corporations or instead (as the case might be) as partnerships, proprietorships, or mere divisions of the companies that own them. Widely regarded as a triumph of common sense and tax simplification for domestic tax purposes, in the international realm the "check-the-box" regulations have been called "one of the worst ideas ever to spring to the minds of usually adroit tax officials at the IRS and Treasury."[12]

The problem arises from the fact that other countries continue to rely on legal form in determining the tax character of a legal entity. Therefore, companies can now easily establish "hybrid branch arrangements," in which a wholly owned corporate subsidiary, from the standpoint of state or national corporate law, is entirely disregarded for United States income tax purposes. This may permit the very same cash flow that a foreign country's tax system regards as deductible (for example, as an interest payment) to be a U.S. tax nonevent, akin to shifting money between the bank accounts of a single company's different branches.

Practitioners use the term *hybrid* to describe entities that different jurisdictions classify differently. They also apply this term to inconsistently characterized financing arrangements. For example, the cash flows under a "hybrid" financial instrument might be a dividend in U.S. eyes but interest for U.K. tax purposes, or a loan payment here but a rental payment or asset acquisition there. The ways in which taxpayers benefit from hybrid arrangements vary considerably. But one relatively simple example involves structuring a payment from abroad to a related party in the United States so that in the source country it is interest, deductible at the country's full statutory rate, but here it is a dividend, taxable at only a 15 percent rate under the revised corporate tax regime that the United States adopted in 2003.

Generalizing the Examples. From a semantic standpoint, the key to all these examples is that many countries' tax systems have broad similarities. To a very large extent, they use common legal concepts, such as corporation, debt, equity, ownership, residence, loan, and lease. Moreover, these common legal concepts often are associated with similar legal consequences. For example, (1) a corporation may be taxed separately from its owners, (2) interest on debt may be deductible while dividends paid to equity holders are not, (3) depreciation deductions may be reserved to owners as compared to lessees, and (4) consolidation between affiliated corporations may be limited to those considered residents.

National tax systems often differ, however, in exactly how they define these shared legal concepts. In some cases, the differences may be pure accidents of history. Or, they may reflect different preferences or circumstances regarding such issues as the choice between determinate black-letter rules and more general standards or the trade-off between offering certainty, on the one hand, and favoring "substance" over mere "form," on the other.

Often, United States tax rules differ from those in other countries by trying harder to apply the principle of "substance over form." Double-dip leases reflect this tendency, since the U.S. rules require a greater inquiry than is internationally typical into indicia of economic ownership. DRCs are an exception, since here the United States looks purely at companies' place of incorporation. And check-the-box is a special case, in which the Treasury threw up its hands on recognizing the failure of earlier efforts to determine which entities were "really" corporate in character.

Countries that have different approaches to defining shared legal concepts do not necessarily disagree with each other about basic tax policy objectives concerning how cross-border transactions should be treated. Rather, they may simply have different administrative preferences or circumstances regarding their own internal tax administrative affairs. Consider this, for example: The United States tries harder than France to look past the formalities of title in a lease agreement and determine which party looks more like the owner in an economic sense, such as by bearing the prospect of gain and the risk of loss. Perhaps the hyperdevelopment of U.S. tax law and practice makes the more difficult inquiry that our approach necessitates easier for people in our system to deal with. Or, perhaps, the French care more than we do about legal certainty. But we need not decide whether their approach is wrong for them, even if we believe that it would be wrong for us. Leaving aside interactions between the two systems, such as double-dip lease transactions, the French pretty much internalize their consequences and we pretty much internalize ours.

Here is why the limited motivation for these legal differences matters. Suppose that France were deliberately making economic policy through its tax rules, such as by subsidizing the airline industry, and we were in a position to reverse the subsidies by giving matching tax penalties to all the companies that were potential beneficiaries. Conceivably, this would increase both worldwide welfare, if the subsidy was inefficient, and our national welfare, by reason of our making money off the reduction in worldwide economic distortion. However, we would be directly interfering with France's economic policy, and one imagines that the French would not be pleased. Indeed, one could easily imagine their retaliating, with possible consequences for both the worldwide and national welfare analyses.

By contrast, in the double-dip lease example, while the government interactions require further consideration, which I offer later, one would not expect the French to have this objection. Rather than making economic policy with regard to the aircraft or leasing industries that is conditioned on enabling double-dip leases, they are likely simply to be making their own administrative judgment, which happens to differ from ours, regarding how they want to administer their own tax system. So, we are not directly defeating their policy judgment if we deny tax benefits from double-dip leases. They still get to administer their tax system in the manner they evidently prefer.

Advantages to Taxpayers of Cross-Border Tax Arbitrages. In part, taxpayers like cross-border tax arbitrages simply because they are there. If being a multinational business entity or having access to worldwide capital markets brings one within reach of an opportunity to make money after tax by engaging in one of these transactions, then of course, one has a reason to do it. And the search for them fits snugly within the broader trend whereby, "over the last two decades, corporate management skills have been progressively refined and successfully applied to a wide variety of previously difficult to control costs . . . [including] corporate tax liabilities."[13]

From the planners' standpoint, moreover, cross-border tax arbitrages may have an important advantage over the arguably abusive corporate tax shelter transactions, such as high-basis, low-value shelters, which I address elsewhere in this volume.[14] A well-designed cross-border tax arbitrage is unexceptionally correct under the application of each country's tax law in isolation. Therefore, American and foreign tax practitioners can offer legal opinions concluding that the transactions work as a matter of their own tax laws, without having to risk running afoul of economic substance or other such requirements. Likewise, government auditors who discover the transactions have no reason to complain about them as a matter of purely domestic law, unless they observe and object to the international aspect.

Are These Really "Arbitrages" or Even "Tax Arbitrages," and Does It Matter?

So far, I have accepted without demurral that the transactions at issue are "cross-border tax arbitrages," simply because that is a term in common use. However, readers with economics backgrounds may already have questioned whether the "arbitrage" label really fits here. They have a point. The term *cross-border tax arbitrage* almost brings to mind the Holy Roman Empire, of which it was famously said that it was neither holy, nor Roman, nor an empire. In this case, the transactions really are cross-border. But they are not actually arbitrages, or even tax arbitrages, as the term has been used in the tax policy literature.

Are They Arbitrages? Economists define *arbitrage* as costlessly buying and selling (or borrowing and lending) the same item at different prices so that one is guaranteed a positive payoff. An arbitrage opportunity therefore provides the equivalent of a risk-free "money pump" for as long as it lasts.[15] The idea that arbitrage is impossible at equilibrium has been called "the one concept that unifies all of finance."[16]

Dual resident companies and double-dip leases are not arbitrages in this sense. They involve a net investment position that happens to receive favorable tax treatment taking into account all countries' tax systems, rather than an offset between positions. Markets do not eliminate them, but rather encourage their continued creation until the point where the marginal tax benefit is no longer worth the marginal nontax cost. Anyone who is accustomed to the standard economic usage of *arbitrage* may therefore find its application here metaphorical at best and misleading at worst.

Are They Tax Arbitrages? The tax policy literature developed a notion of *tax arbitrage* that is broader than the standard finance concept. Might this broader term explain the usage here? A little background may help in elucidating this question. We can start with positions that really are arbitrages in the finance sense.

Within finance, *arbitrage* is certainly not a dirty word. It is simply something that is impossible at equilibrium and the impossibility of which helps to keep financial markets functioning efficiently. In tax policy, however, *arbitrage* is something of a dirty word because, in the formalistic and realization-based system we have, it can result in a catastrophic breakdown of the system.

Suppose, for example, that you hold perfectly hedged long and short positions on the same financial bet, so that your net position is zero, and for tax purposes, without ceasing to be perfectly hedged, you can realize all the losses and none of the gains.[17] There is no natural limit on the amount of tax liability you (and everyone else who could construct the hedge) could eliminate. Indeed, if net losses were refundable, taxpayers could not merely drain the Treasury of positive revenues but generate infinite claims to be paid. Opportunities to engage in this type of tax planning, which Eugene Steuerle dubbed *pure tax arbitrage*, are rife.[18]

The tax system responds to this danger by requiring tax-significant transactions to have economic substance, a nontax business purpose, or to expose the taxpayer to sufficient downside economic risk.[19] So pure tax arbitrage generally does not work for income tax purposes unless it is effectively concealed. One swiftly learns the lesson, however, that departure from it is a matter of degree. At some point, as the hedge between unrealized gain and realized loss positions grows worse, the taxpayer bears enough downside economic risk, or can make enough of a claim to be seeking the upside, to escape the economic substance-type rules.

Tax commentators frequently go on from arbitrages in the finance sense to discuss what Steuerle calls *normal tax arbitrage*.[20] This term refers to the creation by a taxpayer of offsetting long and short positions that are taxed asymmetrically, for example, by pairing an excluded or deferred gain with a currently deductible loss.[21] An example would be borrowing to own a home, and thereby generating excludable imputed rental income along with deductible home mortgage interest expense. This usage of the term *tax arbitrage* is convenient, even though it applies to real net positions that markets do not eliminate, because the technique it describes (while consistent with equilibrium) is important to tax planning and the resulting government responses. What makes the technique important is its usefulness to taxpayers in creating tax losses, without net economic losses, that can be used to shelter positive income and thus to eliminate tax liability across the board.

Cross-border tax arbitrages are not quite this either, however, for one of the same reasons that they are not strict economic arbitrages. Again, they involve a single position, rather than a pair of asymmetrically taxed long and short positions. One might be able to use them in constructing a tax arbitrage, but this merely reflects that their worldwide tax treatment is favorable. Similarly, the income exclusion for a home's imputed rental value is not itself a tax arbitrage but can be used in constructing one.

Why, then, has the term *cross-border tax arbitrage* been used to describe the transactions? In some circles, it might be a rhetorical ploy to cast the transactions, like tax arbitrage in some of the tax policy literature, in an unfavorable light. One can, however, defend it rhetorically or semantically on the ground that the taxpayers in these transactions are "arbitraging" the inconsistencies between two countries' legal rules.

Nothing is inherently wrong with using the term this way if one likes. It is, after all, just a semantic issue. And, perhaps the salience of giving the name *arbitrage* to these instances of clever legal jujitsu is worth the risk of confusion. Yet, one should understand that the sense of semantic inconsistency that underlies the term bears little direct relationship to the reasons why we might be concerned, from a national or worldwide welfare standpoint, about the transactions so described.

From a welfare or efficiency standpoint, the main reason for concern about cross-border tax arbitrages (to abandon further quibbling about the name, simply because it has gained such wide acceptance) is that they involve preferential worldwide tax treatment. Taxpayers who use DRCs or double-dip leases are effectively taxed nowhere on certain worldwide income. The resulting planning opportunities may have undesirable effects on taxpayer behavior and worldwide resource allocation because they violate tax neutrality, a norm that, in some circumstances, promotes efficiency. So, cross-border tax arbitrages are potentially undesirable for the same reasons as single-jurisdiction tax preferences, albeit the cross-border aspect may complicate the national welfare analysis.

As compared with tax preferences generally, cross-border tax arbitrages' distinctive feature, beyond the purely semantic, is their involving what one might call *cross-border tax synergy*, or the use of a cross-border interaction to achieve favorable results not achievable in one country alone. Once we identify the issue this way, we can see that "arbitrage" in the metaphorical sense of exploiting inconsistencies in the application of a shared legal concept (such as corporate residence or tax ownership) is just a means, rather than the end, of ultimate interest.

Semantic inconsistency is neither necessary nor sufficient to achieving cross-border tax synergy. For an example of cross-border tax synergy without the "arbitrage," consider a tax-motivated decision by a U.S. company to acquire as a subsidiary a company in a low-tax country that was formerly an arm's-length trading partner. The idea here might be to shift taxable income to the low-tax country through transfer pricing games, such as claiming an unrealistically high intercompany sales price when the U.S. parent acquires a productive input from the other company. This would not be an "arbitrage" in any sense if the taxpayer reported the same transfer price in both countries, yet it would involve cross-border tax synergy, since income could not otherwise have been shifted for tax purposes from the high-tax to the low-tax country. For an example of legal "arbitrage" (i.e., semantic inconsistency) without the positive tax synergy, consider the case of a DRC that has positive taxable income in both countries.

What is more, the inquiry into whether semantic "arbitrage" exists in a given case may be quite unilluminating. Suppose, for example, that the United Kingdom had the same corporate residence rule as the United States but offered tax benefits to foreign corporations with local headquarters. If the end result were the same as that from being able to claim double deductions by exploiting inconsistent corporate residence rules, it should not matter whether we still regarded this as involving an "arbitrage" between inconsistent applications of the same tax concept.

In practice, developed countries' tax systems are similar enough that cross-border tax synergies often involve exploiting inconsistent definitions of a single term of art.[22] Therefore, looking for cross-border tax arbitrages might be a good strategy for identifying cross-border tax synergies potentially of interest. Yet, we should keep in mind that semantic inconsistency is not inherently something to be concerned about. Taxpayers are not being sneaky or dishonest when they find a clever way to steer through different countries' tax rules; there is no moral duty of worldwide semantic consistency. At the same time, the fact that one can engage in these transactions without shame, if the rules permit them, tells us nothing about whether the rules *should* permit them.

Welfare Implications of Addressing Cross-Border Tax Arbitrages

So What, from the Standpoint of National Tax Policy? Discussions of cross-border tax arbitrage often start from a presumption that tax benefits from the transactions must be allowed unless tax officials can identify a "legitimate objection."[23] Or, we are told that the transactions cannot properly be addressed unless they are demonstrably worse than others that remain permissible,[24] an approach I regard as an open invitation to treat the worst as the enemy of addressing the merely bad. We also may be asked why, in evaluating the U.S. tax treatment, say, of taxpayers with German double-dip leases, we should "be concerned about the rate of tax they are called upon to pay on rental income in Berlin?"[25]

The question is an easy one. The reason we should care about the German tax treatment of a transaction involving American taxpayers is that it may affect us. Other countries' tax rules may influence our taxpayers' incentives. Such rules are therefore likely to affect the investments Americans make and the resources they spend on tax planning. Their pretax and aftertax income may be affected by foreign tax rules, and so may our tax collections. Effects of this sort are normally considered to lie well within a government's reasonable areas of concern. Indeed, if we did not care about them, it is hard to see why anyone would want to consider granting foreign tax credits.

The foreign tax treatment of a given transaction involving one's own taxpayers is merely a factual input, like any other, to the question of how the different rules that one might select would affect national welfare. Indeed, the only difference that comes to mind between this input and any other is that this one may tend (albeit not uniquely) to raise issues of strategic interaction between different countries. For example, if the Germans notice that we expressly respond to their tax rules, then perhaps they will be more likely to respond in turn to ours. Such strategic interactions are always relevant to the consequences of adopting a given policy and, accordingly, should be taken into account here, just as in any other setting.

For analytical convenience, however, I start my evaluation of cross-border tax arbitrages from a national welfare standpoint by assuming that the United States response to a given cross-border tax arbitrage is entirely unilateral, in the sense of not affecting other countries' decisions. I then turn to issues of strategic interaction.

Unilateral Responses to Cross-Border Tax Arbitrage (and Other Cross-Border Tax Synergies). A good starting point, in evaluating the United States tax issues raised by double-dip leases and DRCs, is to ask why we allow income tax deductions, such as for depreciation or a consolidated group member's losses, in the first place. The fact that allowing these deductions may improve the accuracy with which the tax system measures net income is merely a means. The end, presumably, is to improve the efficiency and distributional consequences of our income tax (and government rules generally) relative to the case where the deductions are not allowed. For example, suppose there were a proposal to tax supermarkets on their gross sales receipts, without allowing them to recover costs of goods sold and operating expenses, while all other businesses continued to be taxed as at present.[26] It seems likely that this proposal would inefficiently discourage supermarkets relative to other business undertakings.[27] It also might prompt costly avoidance responses by supermarkets (for example, purporting to be a middleman that does not actually own the goods it sells and therefore is taxable only on the spread).

Now suppose we learned that, for some odd reason, allowing supermarkets the same sorts of deductions as any other business would actually reduce efficiency and equity. Then, the case for taxing them on their gross sales receipts might be a good one after all. Denying them all deductions and other cost recovery would have two compelling advantages. First, it would (by express hypothesis) directly increase efficiency and equity. Second, if the gross sales receipts tax on supermarkets raised revenue (despite any possible Laffer curve effect) and the government had fixed revenue goals, then adoption of this tax would reduce the need to induce further economic distortion by levying higher taxes in some other setting.

Assuming for now that other countries do not address cross-border tax arbitrages, this seemingly absurd hypothetical offers a compelling way to look at DRCs and double-dip leases. Allowing corporate groups to deduct one member's losses against another's net income and providing cost recovery with respect to depreciable business assets may generally be good ideas. However, if a foreign government is kind enough to provide deductions for these items, then why should we do so as well? Doubling the deductions provides a worldwide tax preference for these transactions that may increase economic distortion by inducing American taxpayers to choose investments with inferior pretax returns. It may also cost the United States tax revenues that would end up being replaced through distortive taxes on something else. Accordingly, just as in the supermarket hypothetical, denying DRC and double-dip lease deductions is potentially a win-win proposition from a policy standpoint.[28]

Likewise, suppose Bill Gates announced that, as a service to the United States economy, he would be willing to offer cash to anyone who had a valid business deduction, equaling the tax benefit that they would get from claiming the deduction. Would there be any reason not to let him relieve the United States Treasury of the fiscal burden of allowing deductions? Why not take advantage of the fact that he was now permitting us to levy a tax on gross income that would have the same economic effects as a tax on net income without his help?

Suppose one disagreed with the specifics of this analysis, believing, for example, that selectively available double cost recovery for airplanes improves efficiency. That view would not require disagreement with the national welfare-based framework for analysis of cross-border tax arbitrages I advocate here. It would merely suggest applying the framework in a given case to reach a different conclusion.

My analysis also should not be interpreted as suggesting that cross-border tax arbitrages should generally be disallowed, even in the purely unilateral setting where there are no strategic interactions with other countries. Just like the evaluation of tax benefits in the purely domestic setting, the issue calls, rather, for a case-by-case analysis. Suppose, for example, a particular cross-border tax arbitrage serves mainly to mitigate domestic double taxation of corporate income. This might be a laudable result if one generally favors corporate integration. Finally, I intend no implication that only positive or pro-taxpayer cross-border tax synergies should be addressed. Those unfavorable to multinational businesses merit evaluation on national welfare grounds as well, and their imposing a kind of tax penalty relative to purely domestic activity may frequently count against them.[29]

In the discussion thus far, I glossed over just how broadly applicable this mode of analysis may be. Since it looks exclusively at the national welfare effects of unilateral deduction denial by the United States, it is not limited to cases of cross-border tax arbitrage. (And this should come as no surprise, once I have dismissed as merely semantic the question of whether two countries' legal rules are being inconsistently "arbitraged" against each other.) Indeed, it is not even limited to cases of cross-border tax synergy. Rather, the set of cases in which the analysis could apply is potentially close to unlimited.

Suppose, for example, that the United Kingdom offers what we consider unduly favorable tax treatment to the oil industry or otherwise favors that industry through government spending or special regulatory exemptions. It is conceivable, in such a case (again, assuming unilateral action), that the United States could increase national and also worldwide welfare by providing an income tax penalty designed to reverse those undue U.K. benefits whenever they were enjoyed by a U.S. taxpayer.

More generally, one could imagine the United States scouring the world in quest of inefficient subsidies it is in a position to reverse, to its own national benefit and perhaps that of the world economy, through offsetting income tax (or other) penalties. Pushed to this extreme, however, one may begin to question whether such an enterprise might end up proving misguided and counterproductive. In particular, one might wonder what other countries would think about this course of action, and how they would respond to it.

The point this makes, however, is simply that unilateral action by the United States cannot be assumed. Particularly (although not uniquely), if we are making money by effectively reversing other countries' deliberate economic policies, those countries might respond by doing things we would not like. And such a possibility must be considered even in the case of a cross-border tax arbitrage that likely reflects an inadvertent interaction resulting from slight differences in tax rules, rather than the other country's considered economic policy.

To the extent we can act unilaterally, however, there are likely to be win-win cases where the United States does well by doing good. That is, we may be able to raise revenue by reducing inefficiencies in the national and world economies. Responding to such opportunities (for example, by denying U.S. benefits to DRCs or double-dip leases, if this would increase national welfare, as I tentatively suggested) potentially offers us a result that is even better than free money. Leaving this (better than) free money on the table, by not responding to cross-border tax arbitrages where a response is in our national interest, would be foolish.

Strategic Interactions between Countries' Tax Systems. Again, my assumption in the previous section that the United States can act unilaterally was just an analytically convenient starting point. Other countries are always capable of responding to what we do. Moreover, when we adopt policies that respond to or rely on their legal rules, they may be especially likely to pay attention. For example, deliberately offsetting their subsidies with penalties might lead to retaliation, although in any given case, we might conceivably get away with it (or benefit on balance despite the response).

How should we generally expect other countries to respond when we deny U.S. tax benefits to a multinational enterprise by reason of a cross-border tax arbitrage? No less than in the subsidy reversal case, in practice, this might amount to an open invitation to the other country to reconsider its rule in light of ours. We have raised the subject of the rules' interacting effects, after all, and (in a case like the DRC or double-dip lease) denied deductions specifically because the other country is or may be granting them.

There is, however, a significant difference from the case of reversing other countries' deliberate subsidies. In the double-dip lease example, France presumably is not aiming to maximize the worldwide tax subsidy to airplanes. Nor is it likely to be raising the tricolor in support of the proposition that depreciation deductions ought always to go to legal owners. Its aim, rather, may simply be to implement a net income concept by allowing depreciation, while defining tax ownership in the manner that it happens to find convenient administratively. We might not, therefore, defeat French policy goals by denying our own depreciation deductions in cases of duplicative tax ownership. A similar analysis might apply to DRCs, the U.K. corporate residence rules, and the U.K. treatment of consolidated groups.

Suppose the United States addressed both these cross-border tax arbitrages by denying the duplicated deductions and, for some reason, France and the United Kingdom were entirely unable to change their own rules. Under this circumstance, both countries might well be grateful to us for stepping in. Deduction denial by the United States might conceivably induce their own residents to make better pretax investments and spend less money on tax planning. France and the United Kingdom also might conceivably gain revenue if their taxpayers engaged in fewer of these transactions by reason of the U.S. response.

Now, however, suppose (a lot more reasonably) that France and the United Kingdom are perfectly capable of enacting their own responses to these transactions. Even if they are sympathetic to eliminating double deductibility, they may wonder why the United States should capture the entire direct fiscal benefit. Why should we get to free-ride on the fact that they offer deductions that both sides agree should be taken only once, when they could just as easily free-ride on us? They might further think of us as administrative freeriders, if we conditioned our denial of tax benefits on findings of corporate residence or tax ownership made by their tax systems.

In sum, by responding unilaterally with deduction denial, the United States could be viewed as aggressively grabbing nearly all the available joint surplus from a bilateral monopoly (involving the welfare gain that the countries can reap by coordinating their tax rules). Other countries might rationally expect to benefit from demanding a greater share of the joint surplus, even at the risk of destroying it all. Threats and chicken games are, after all, a common feature of bargaining over the division of surplus.

One should not be entirely surprised, therefore, if the United Kingdom enacts its own duplicative (for U.S.-U.K. dual residents) response to the DRC problem.[30] The potential for double nondeductibility in the case of U.S.-U.K. dual residents has begun to prompt taxpayer complaints, although initial efforts to address it through the treaty process resulted only in an agreement that the two countries' competent authorities should reach some agreement.[31]

When both of a DRC's resident countries respond with overlapping deduction disallowance rules, the distortion may be less than that from double deductibility, since incurring DRC losses is to some extent elective. Companies can deliberately plan to create DRCs that are assured of incurring tax losses due to intergroup game playing, and they can try to avoid having DRCs that are profitable for tax purposes. Nonetheless, double disallowance may amount to overkill given the possibility of cases where one has business reasons for establishing a DRC that is making risky investments with the possibility of loss. Even if both the United States and the United Kingdom would benefit, no matter what the other country did, from unilaterally denying the deductions, it is conceivable that they would do better still by coordinating their rules to allow the deductions a total of once. This might involve splitting the deductions 50-50, or through any other objective, even if arbitrary, formula.

To date, double-dip leases present the opposite scenario. Neither the United States nor the foreign countries that base tax ownership rules exclusively on legal title have thus far sought to claim what is arguably free money on the table by denying duplicative deductions. So, here, there may be collective "underkill" rather than overkill.

These two examples help show that achieving desirable coordination between countries' responses to cross-border tax arbitrage is not all that easy. The problem may have less to do with ineluctable disagreement between sovereigns, such as concerning the division of joint surplus, than with inattention, competing priorities, and domestic political considerations.

The U.S. Treasury, for example, might have little inclination to devote its scarce human resources to coordinating our responses to cross-border tax arbitrages with those of other countries, even if it had the authority to do so. It faced intense domestic political opposition even when proposing responses that would give the United States 100 percent of the direct fiscal benefit. And, even if there were more domestic support in principle to devising joint responses with other countries, obtaining congressional approval via a treaty or legislation might be quite difficult. Members of the tax committees in both houses of Congress often have agendas of their own. They also have a collective institutional interest in objecting to the use of the treaty process (which involves only the

Senate, under the jurisdiction of the Senate Foreign Relations Committee) to implement substantive tax law changes.

Yet, all this need not deter the United States from responding unilaterally to cross-border tax arbitrages. Other countries may frequently be slow to act, and taxpayer self-help through tax planning and the exertion of political pressure may mitigate instances (like the DRC) of bilateral overkill. Unilateral action should not be undertaken, of course, in cases where it involves bad policy standing alone. Yet, opportunities to free-ride on other countries' willingness to offer deductions (or allow business income to escape their source-based taxes) may often be worth exploiting, on the ground that they are likely to combine doing well with doing good.

Where unilateral action would not be good policy, this can be argued on the merits of the particular case (or in more broadly applicable terms). One might argue, for example, that preventing United States taxpayers from exploiting a given planning opportunity available to foreign investors would in some way disadvantage us. Or, one might argue that, given the arbitrariness and growing avoidability of our corporate residence rules, there is no point in seeking increased foreign-source tax collections from U.S. corporations. Still another argument might be that, given the existence of various negative cross-border tax synergies, permitting multinational businesses to exploit favorable synergies serves on balance to reduce tax distortion.

The great virtue of such arguments is that, whether right or wrong, they address the right set of issues. They thus advance a debate that has too often focused on claims that other countries' tax rules (despite their clear effects on us) are, for some unstated reason, none of our business.

A Broader Perspective on Cross-Border Tax Arbitrage and Tax Harmonization

Do the issues raised by cross-border tax arbitrage offer any broader lessons regarding either the desirability or the feasibility of general tax harmonization? On the question of desirability, the fact that neither tax harmonization nor tax competition is always best has been widely recognized. "At that level of generality, one might as well ask whether government is good or bad."[32] One rough rule of thumb that may provide guidance, however, is the view that harmonizing income tax bases often makes sense even if tax competition with respect to rates is retained or indeed encouraged.[33]

Eliminating cross-border tax arbitrages resembles tax base harmonization but with an important difference. It does not require that different countries actually adopt the same rules. Suppose France and the United States have difficulty in agreeing to the same tax ownership rule, whether out of national pride, because they face different administrative trade-offs, or because changing one's existing rule is costly to each country in some way. A rule eliminating duplicative deductions for double-dip leases, whether adopted unilaterally or bilaterally and no matter how the revenues were divided, would not require either country to agree which rule was best or depart from its own preferred and settled administrative practice. Accordingly, some of the arguments against tax base harmonization do not apply to proposals to move toward elimination of cross-border tax arbitrages.

A broader point concerns how, in this setting and others, international institutions might be developed to facilitate desirable international cooperation in tax matters. Some commentators have urged the creation of a "GATT for Taxes" or a "World Tax Organization," analogous to existing institutions that oversee international trade.[34] An admitted problem, however, is the lack of any obvious reference point akin to free trade. Even among experts, there is no international consensus regarding such matters as what sort of tax to levy at the corporate level and how to relate that tax to the taxation of shareholders.

A multilateral tax organization need not take as its mission the creation of worldwide tax base uniformity, however. Instead, it can aim to coordinate international cooperation where that would be to mutual advantage but is impeded by transaction costs. Eliminating cross-border tax arbitrages and other tax synergies through the reciprocal reduction of duplicated or poorly coordinated tax benefits is one possible application. A second, the flip side of this enterprise, might be reining in countries' occasional inclination to adopt narrow definitions of foreign source income and thereby "cheat" at the margin in offering foreign tax credits or exemption. Furthering international cooperation in tax collection, administration, and information gathering might be a third undertaking.

Unilateral action by the United States to deny tax benefits in cases of cross-border tax arbitrage might seem a long way from this endpoint. And, indeed, such unilateral action mixes the competitive with the cooperative, since while potentially aiding countries that are slow to act, it does so by grabbing the entire direct fiscal benefit that others might want to share. Yet, addressing cross-border tax arbitrage has at least the potential to help everyone move in the direction of greater worldwide cooperation, while possibly advancing purely national ends in the here and now.

Notes

Chapter 1: Are Corporate Tax Shelters an "Abuse" That Should Be Stopped?

1. See Sheryl Stratton, "Treasury Responds to Critics of Corporate Tax Shelter Proposals," *Tax Notes* 84 (1999): 17.

2. From *Gregory v. Helvering*, 69 F.2d 809, 810 (2nd Cir. 1934), aff'd, 293 U.S. 465 (1935).

3. See Joseph Bankman, "The New Market in Corporate Tax Shelters," *Tax Notes* 83 (1999): 1777, noting that the typical corporate tax shelter "is likely to be shut down by legislative or administrative change soon after it is detected."

4. See United States Senate, Permanent Subcommittee on Investigations, "U.S. Tax Shelter Industry: The Role of Accountants, Lawyers, and Financial Professionals—Four KPMG Case Studies: Flip, Opis, Blips, and SC2," report prepared by the minority staff (Washington, D.C., 2003), available at http://www.ecommerce.tax.com/Official_docs/tax_shelter_study.htm.

5. See Mihir Desai, "The Divergence between Book Income and Tax Income," in *Tax Policy and the Economy*, vol. 17, ed. James M. Poterba (Cambridge, Mass.: MIT Press, 2003); George Plesko, "An Evaluation of Alternative Measures of Corporate Tax Rates," *Journal of Accounting and Economics* 35, no. 2 (April 2003): 201.

6. See Edward D. Kleinbard, "Corporate Tax Shelters and Corporate Tax Management," *Tax Executive* 51 (1999): 231.

7. On the shifting culture of tax practice, see Bankman, "The New Market."

8. For just a few examples of articles exploring the rules versus standards issue in the corporate tax shelter debate, see David Weisbach, "An Economic Analysis of Anti-Tax Avoidance Doctrines," working paper, 2d

series, no. 99 (Chicago: University of Chicago Law School, 2000);
Kleinbard, "Corporate Tax Shelters"; James P. Holden, "Dealing with the
Aggressive Corporate Tax Shelter Problem," *Tax Notes* 82 (1999): 707;
Kenneth W. Gideon, "Tax Law Works Best when the Rules are Clear," *Tax
Notes* 81 (1998): 999; and New York State Bar Association Section on
Taxation, "Comments on the Administration's Corporate Tax Shelter
Proposals," reprinted in *Tax Notes* 83 (1999): 879.

9. 113 T.C. 214 (1999), rev'd, 277 F.3d 778 (2001). In *IES Industries,
Inc. v. United States*, 253 F.3d 350 (8th Cir. 2000), the Eighth Circuit
similarly reversed a lower court decision in favor of the government, in
a largely identical transaction.

10. I criticized the Fifth Circuit's reversal of the Tax Court decision in
Compaq in Daniel N. Shaviro and David A. Weisbach, "The Fifth Circuit
Gets It Wrong in *Compaq v. Commissioner*," *Tax Notes* 94 (2002): 511.

11. Internal Revenue Code section 1211, limiting deductible capital
losses to the amount of capital gains (generally plus $3,000 for individuals).

12. I.R.C. section 904, generally permitting foreign tax credits only to
the extent that they offset the United States tax liability on specified foreign source income.

13. I.R.C. section 469.

14. I.R.C. section 163(d).

15. See, e.g., Daniel N. Shaviro, "Selective Limitations on Tax
Benefits," *University of Chicago Law Review* 56 (1989): 1189; Shaviro,
"Rethinking Anti-Tax Shelter Rules: Protecting the Earned Income Tax
Base," *Taxes* 46 (1993): 859.

16. As variants of an economic substance requirement, I include such
related common law doctrines as business purpose, substance over
form, and step transaction doctrine. For useful discussion of the fea-
tures and differences between these various doctrines, see, e.g., Joseph
Bankman, "The Economic Substance Doctrine, 2000," *Southern
California Law Review* 74 (2000): 5; David Hariton, "Sorting Out the
Tangle of Economic Substance," *Tax Lawyer* 52 (1999): 235; Kleinbard,
"Corporate Tax Shelters."

17. Eugene C. Steuerle, *Taxes, Loans, and Inflation* (Washington, D.C.:
Brookings Institution, 1985), 60.

18. 430 F.2d 1185 (5th Cir. 1970), cert. denied, 401 U.S. 939 (1971).

19. I ignore the possibility that risk penalties under the income tax
serve corporate governance aims by countering management's incentive
to make risky bets in which shareholders have the upside and creditors
(due to default risk) have the downside.

20. As I discuss later, however, it is not entirely clear why a company such as Compaq (or at least its shareholders) should object to the risk of holding other stock, which at the shareholder level might increase international diversification.

21. I.R.C. section 465.

22. I.R.C. section 469.

23. I.R.C. section 1091.

24. I emphasize "corporate" tax shelters because they have received so much recent attention. Similar transactions involving individuals may raise similar tax policy issues, and various practitioners have told me anecdotally that they are on the rise.

25. See Bankman, "The New Market," 1777, for a fuller definition of corporate tax shelters.

26. However, in the companion article in this volume, I discuss transactions that instead "arbitrage" (as it is commonly but loosely said) differences between two or more countries' tax rules.

27. This is the ex-dividend price one would expect if the marginal purchaser of A's stock cannot claim foreign tax credits (e.g., by reason of being tax exempt). Since a tax-exempt holder places zero value on the $3 foreign tax credit one accrues by receiving a dividend that has borne a $3 withholding tax, it would pay $7 more for the stock immediately before than immediately after the owner thereof is entitled to receive a $7 net dividend payout.

28. Absent the schedular rule limiting the use of foreign tax credits to offset the U.S. tax on foreign source income, in principle all income tax liability could be limited by *Compaq*-style transactions if (as is perhaps unlikely) there continued to be enough foreign stock that changed in price ex dividend only by the after-withholding-tax amount of the dividend.

29. See I.R.C. section 351.

30. I.R.C. section 988.

31. If done with "nonqualified preferred stock," the transaction would also fail under I.R.C. section 351(g)(3).

32. F presumably has $95 million of gain at this time, from the deemed sale of an asset with zero basis for $95 million, but at least it got the losses first, and perhaps it can, at this point, arrange additional loss transactions.

33. See, e.g., Revenue Procedure 75-21, 1975-1 C.B. 715, setting forth guidelines for the minimum economic substance of a leasing transaction on which the IRS will issue a favorable advance ruling.

34. See David Hariton, "Tax Benefits, Tax Administration, and Legislative Intent," *Tax Lawyer* 53 (2000): 579.

35. Despite the "silly leasing" character of the current rules, their economic substance component may be strong enough to deter significant numbers of potential sale-leaseback transactions. The enactment in 1981 and repeal in 1982 of "safe harbor leasing" rules, which expressly had no economic substance requirement whatsoever, was estimated by the Joint Committee on Taxation to have significant revenue consequences.

36. See, e.g., Harry Grubert and Jack Mutti, *Taxing International Business Income: Dividend Exemption versus the Current System* (Washington, D.C.: AEI Press, 2001); James R. Hines, "The Case against Deferral: A Deferential Reconsideration," *National Tax Journal* 52 (1999): 385.

37. Daniel N. Shaviro, "Economic Substance, Corporate Tax Shelters, and the *Compaq* Case," *Tax Notes* 88 (2000): 221.

Chapter 2: More Revenues, Less Distortion? Responding to Cross-Border Tax Arbitrage

1. Daniel N. Shaviro, "Are Corporate Tax Shelters an 'Abuse' That Should Be Stopped?" pages 1–26 of this volume.

2. See Ronald Coase, "The Problem of Social Cost," *Journal of Law and Economics* 3 (1960): 1–44.

3. See IRS Notice 98-11, 1998-1 C.B. 433 (proposing to limit certain cross-border tax benefits); IRS Notice 98-35, 1998-2 C.B. 34 (withdrawing Notice 98-11). On the controversiality of Notice 98-11, see, for example, Robert A. Jacobs, "NYSBA Criticizes Treasury's Subpart F Study," *2002 Tax Notes Today*, no. 8-20 (2002).

4. See, for example, Revenue Ruling 2002-69, 2002-44 I.R.B. 760, challenging cross-border lease-in, lease-out (LILO) arrangements, and revising but not abandoning the challenge to LILOs in Revenue Ruling 99-14, 199-1 C.B. 835.

5. A full welfare analysis requires considering distributional as well as efficiency issues, but distributional issues may not be of central importance in comparing the taxation of multinationals to that of purely domestic business enterprises.

6. H. David Rosenbloom, "International Tax Arbitrage and the International Tax System," *Tax Law Review* 53 (2000): 139.

7. Ibid., 151.

8. See, for example, ibid., 142; Philip R. West, "Foreign Law in U.S. International Taxation: The Search for Standards," *Florida Tax Review* 3 (1996): 171.

9. Strictly speaking, consolidation is the U.S. approach, whereas the United Kingdom permits losses to be surrendered by one member of the resident group to another. For present purposes, however, the two approaches are effectively the same.

10. Internal Revenue Code, section 1503(d).

11. See David R. Hardy, "A Company without a Country: The Dual Consolidated Loss Regime," *Tax Notes* 84 (1999): 756. The U.K. rule excludes dual resident companies from the U.K. consolidated group, rather than specifically addressing losses like the U.S. rule (ibid.).

12. Martin A. Sullivan, "Tax Amnesty International: Relief for Prodigal Profits," *Tax Notes* 99 (2003): 606–7.

13. Edward D. Kleinbard, "Corporate Tax Shelters and Corporate Tax Management," *Tax Executive* 51 (1999): 234.

14. See Shaviro, "Are Corporate Tax Shelters an 'Abuse'?" 12–17.

15. Philip H. Dybvig and Stephen A. Ross, "Arbitrage," in *The New Palgrave: Finance*, eds. John Eatwell, Murray Milgate, and Peter Newman (New York: Stockton Press, 1989), 57.

16. Ibid., 67.

17. In fact, the straddle rules of Internal Revenue Code section 1092 prevent taxpayers from deducting their losses in these circumstances, but the example provides a convenient illustration.

18. C. Eugene Steuerle, *Taxes, Loans, and Inflation: How the Nation's Wealth Becomes Misallocated* (Washington, D.C.: The Brookings Institution, 1985), 59–60. For example, the tax system often distinguishes between fixed and contingent returns, taxing the former on a current accrual basis but awaiting realization for the latter. However, two or more contingent returns that offset each other can equal a fixed position. Taxpayers can therefore use offsetting contingent positions to create "synthetic" fixed positions, potentially permitting the creation of perfect arbitrages that generate unlimited losses (with offsetting gains being assigned, if necessary, to tax exempts). See Alvin C. Warren, "Financial Contract Innovation and Income Tax Policy," *Harvard Law Review* 107 (1993): 460–92.

19. See Shaviro, "Are Corporate Tax Shelters an 'Abuse'?" 7–8; Shaviro, "Risk-Based Rules and the Taxation of Capital Income," *Tax Law Review* 50 (1995): 643–724.

20. See Steuerle, *Taxes, Loans, and Inflation*, 59–60.

21. See, e.g., David F. Bradford, *Untangling the Income Tax* (Cambridge, Mass.: Harvard University Press, 1986), 39–40; Steuerle, *Taxes, Loans, and Inflation*, 57–61.

22. There also are negative cross-border tax synergies resulting from such inconsistencies that are to the taxpayer's detriment. A prominent example concerns the treatment of interest expense incurred by U.S. multinationals. See Daniel N. Shaviro, "Does More Sophisticated Mean Better? A Critique of Alternative Approaches to Sourcing the Interest Expense of American Multinationals," *Tax Law Review* 54 (2001): 353.

23. West, "Foreign Law in U.S. International Taxation," 171.

24. Rosenbloom, "International Tax Arbitrage," 148.

25. Ibid., 151. For an important exception to the style of analysis I criticize here, see Reuven S. Avi-Yonah, "Commentary," *Tax Law Review* 53 (2000): 167.

26. The distinction between the tax treatment of supermarkets and other undertakings is needed because they would not be relatively disadvantaged, say, by a comprehensive retail sales tax.

27. The proposal's distributional effects depend on how it affects pretax returns. It is plausible that, as Boris Bittker put it, all the inequity would be converted into inefficiency by taxpayer exit from the supermarket business. Boris I. Bittker, "Equity, Efficiency, and the Income Tax: Do Misallocations Drive Out Inequities?" *San Diego Law Review* 16 (1979): 735.

28. The actual rationale for the U.S. rule limiting the use of DRC losses by U.S. consolidated groups, as stated in the 1986 legislative history, emphasized "competitiveness" rather than the efficiency concerns that I would find more persuasive.

29. Shaviro, "Does More Sophisticated Mean Better?" is generally critical of a negative cross-border tax synergy arising from differences between United States and foreign rules for "sourcing" interest expense.

30. Germany also recently enacted a loss disallowance rule for DRCs, although several other countries (such as Australia and the Netherlands) that employ a headquarters approach to corporate residence have not. See Eugen Bogenschuetz and Kelly Wright, "Change Begets More Change: The Permanent German Tax Reform," *Tax Notes International* 25 (2002): 1125.

31. See Philip R. West, "Highlights of the New U.S.-U.K. Tax Treaty," *Tax Notes* 92 (2001): 663.

32. Daniel N. Shaviro, "Some Observations Concerning Multi-Jurisdictional Tax Competition," in *Regulatory Competition and Economic*

Integration: Comparative Perspectives, eds. Daniel Esty and Damien Geradin (New York: Oxford University Press, 2001), 67.

33. See, e.g., Daniel N. Shaviro, *Federalism in Taxation: The Case for Greater Uniformity* (Washington, D.C.: AEI Press, 1993).

34. See, e.g., Jack M. Mintz, "The Role of Allocation in a Globalized Corporate Income Tax," working paper 98-134 (Washington, D.C.: International Monetary Fund, 1998); Vito Tanzi, *Taxation in an Integrating World* (Washington, D.C.: Brookings Institution Press, 1995).

About the Author

Daniel N. Shaviro is the Wayne Perry Professor of Taxation at New York University Law School and a visiting scholar at the American Enterprise Institute. His research has mainly emphasized income tax policy, government transfers, budgetary measures, social insurance, and entitlements reform. He is the author of *Do Deficits Matter?* (1997), *When Rules Change: An Economic and Political Analysis of Transition Relief and Retroactivity* (2000), *Making Sense of Social Security Reform* (2000), and *Who Should Pay for Medicare?* (2004), all published by the University of Chicago Press.